China
phrasebook

||||||||||||||||||

✓ P9-CJM-569

175

lonely planet

China Phrasebook

Published by
Lonely Planet Publications
PO Box 88, South Yarra, Victoria 3141, Australia
PO Box 2001A, Berkeley, CA 94702, USA

Printed by
Colorcraft, Hong Kong

Design & Illustrations by
Graham Imeson & Fiona Boyes

Typesetting by
Ann Logan

First published
June 1985

National Library of Australia
Cataloguing in Publication

China Phrasebook.

ISBN 0 908086 82 2.

1. Chinese language – Conversation and phrase books – English. I. Title.

495.1'83

Copyright © Lonely Planet, 1985

Contents

Pronunciation

There are many dialects in China, including Cantonese, the one most commonly heard in Australia. But it is Mandarin Chinese, or *putonghua*, that this phrasebook tells you how to say the things you need to say in Chinese. *Putonghua*, based on the Beijing dialect, is the official language of the country and is the one spoken by the largest number of Chinese. Of course not all Chinese speak it in the way it should be spoken, and you should be prepared for a range of regional accents differing more widely that standard English does from Scottish, Cockney or American.

Tones For speakers of English the sounds of Chinese are quite easy to reproduce. There are relatively few of them and many of them have English equivalents. What is a little more difficult is pronouncing the words in the right tone. In Chinese there are many words which are pronounced in exactly the same way, but mean something quite different. The way in which the words are distinguished is by the tone which is used. Were it not for the distinctions offered by these tones, spoken Chinese would be almost unintelligible.

For example, it's no good just saying *tang* if you're ordering soup in a restaurant. Unless you pronounced the word in an unchanging high pitch, you could find yourself being given sugar, also *tang*, but pronounced in a rising tone.

6 Pronunciation

There are four basic tones in putonghua:

First tone – high-level —
Second tone – rising /
Third tone – falling-rising ‿
Fourth tone – falling \

A visual representation of these will look something like this:

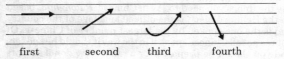

first   second   third   fourth

Every syllable is pronounced in one of these four tones, but a word can lose its tone when it is unstressed. When that happens the syllable is left unmarked. Such syllables are pronounced quickly and lightly, in no particular tone.

Vowels

a	as 'a' in 'father'
ai	as 'uy' in 'buy'
ao	as 'ow' in 'now'
e	as 'ur' in 'fur'
ei	as 'ay' in 'day'
i	as 'ee' in 'see'. When **i** follows the consonants **c**, **ch**, **r**, **s**, **sh**, **z** or **zh** it is silent but you prolong the sound you make with the preceding consonant.
ian	as 'yen'
ie	as 'ere' in 'here'
iu	as in 'you'
o	as in 'awe'

ou	as 'ow' in 'low'
u	as 'oo' in 'woo'
ü	as the French 'tu', or the German 'für'. Place your lips as if you were going to whistle, and say 'ee', without moving them.

Consonants

c	as 'ts' in 'cats'
ch	as 'tr' in 'true'
g	as 'g' in 'go'
h	a guttural sound like the 'ch' in 'loch', or in the German 'ich'.
q	as 'ch' in 'cheese'
r	as in English, but much softer, so that it sounds almost like the 's' in 'measure'. Say 'r', but touch the roof of your mouth with the tip of your tongue.
sh	as 'shr' in 'shriek'
x	as 'sc' in 'science'
y	as 'y' in 'yes'
z	as 'ds' in 'fads'
zh	as 'dr' in 'drool'

All the other consonants are pronounced pretty close to their English equivalents.

All the words written using the roman alphabet in this book are written in the official *pinyin* transcript. This system replaced the Wade-Giles writing system some time ago, and is the one you will now see on Chinese signs, next to the Chinese characters. You can use this pronunciation guide to read these words but when you are wandering around China don't make the mistake of thinking that because you can read the transcript the Chinese can too.

Grammar

The sentence

The sentence in spoken Chinese is usually short. There are no verb conjugations as we know them. Consequently there are no variations in verb form between singular and plural. The verb does not change form at all, but sometimes short words are added to it for emphasis or to show that something is in the past.

I go to Shanghai.
Wǒ qù Shànghǎi.　　　　　我去上海

Shanghai (is) very big.
Shànghǎi hěn dà.　　　　　上海很大

How much does it cost? (Lit. How much money?)
Duōshǎo qián.　　　　　　多少钱

I have eaten. (Lit. Eat, and a past tense marker *le*).
Chī le.　　　　　　　　　吃了

(It's) not cheap.
Bù piányi.　　　　　　　　不便宜

He is fond of Chinese food
Tā ài chī Zhōngguó cài.　　他爱吃中国菜

Negatives

To make a sentence negative, put the verb after these words.

bù	not	不
méi	did not, has not	沒
méiyǒu	there is not, there are not	沒有

8

bié   don't   别

For example,

I'm not going to Shanghai.

Wǒ bù qù Shànghǎi.   我不去上海

I didn't go to Shanghai.

Wǒ méi qù Shànghǎi.   我没去上海

I have no money.

Wǒ méiyǒu qián.   我没有钱

Don't make a noise.

Bié chǎo.   别吵

Yes, No

To say yes in answer to a question you repeat the verb. To say no, you repeat the verb, placing *bu*, the negative, in front of it.

Are you going to Shanghai?

Nǐ qù Shànghǎi ma?   你去上海吗

Yes. (I go)

Wǒ qù.   我去

No. (I don't go)

Wǒ bù qù.   我不去

Pronouns

I/me	*wǒ*	我
you	*nǐ*	你
he/him	*tā*	他
she/her	*tā*	她
we/us	*wǒmen*	我们
you (pl)	*nǐmen*	你们
they/them	*tāmen*	他们
it	*tā*	它

this	zhè	这
these	zhèi xiē	这些
that	nèi ge	那个
those	nèi xiē	那些

Questions

who	shéi	Nǐ shì shéi?	你是谁
		Who are you?	
which	nǎ yī ge	Nǎ yī ge piányi?	哪一个便宜
		Which is cheaper?	
what	shénme	Zhèi shì shénme?	这是什么
		What is this?	
where	nǎr	Tā qù nǎr?	他去哪儿
		Where is he going?	
how	zěnme	Zěnme qù?	怎么去
		How (do I) go?	
when	shénme	Shénme shíhòu qù Shànghǎi?	
	shíhòu	When (do you) go to Shanghai?	
			什么时候去上海

To make a statement a question, add the word *ma* to the end of it, and raise the intonation of your voice.

He goes to Shanghai.

    Tā qù Shànghǎi.   他去上海

Is he going to Shanghai?

    Tā qù Shànghǎi ma?   他去上海吗

A third way of forming a question is by placing the verb and the negative of the verb together. This is a bit like saying 'or not?' in English. For example,

Are you going to Shanghai? (Lit. You go not go Shanghai?)

    Nǐ qù bu qù Shanghai?   你去不去上海

Do you have money (or not)?

Nǐ yǒu méiyǒu qián? 你有没有钱

(Lit. You have not have money?)

To say 'or', as in 'tea or coffee', you use the word *háishì*. Use it in exactly the same way as you would in English by placing it between the two choices.

Are you going to Shanghai or Beijing?

Nǐ qù Shànghǎi háishì qù Běijīng? 你去上海还是去北京

Measure words

In Chinese the same word is used, whether the thing you are talking about is singular or plural. Usually the context will show whether you are talking about one or more things. When you are talking about an exact quantity, like two, three or four things, you need to make use of a measure word, or a counter. This is also true when you are using the pronouns 'this','that', 'these', 'those'. A measure word says something about the kind of thing you are counting. There are different measure words for different kinds of nouns. They are placed between the number or pronoun and the noun, and work in the same way as words like 'flock' and 'herd' in the expressions 'a herd of cattle' or 'a flock of sheep'. There is a general measure word, *ge*, which may be applied to all nouns, so if you can't remember the one you want, or you don't know which it is, you will be perfectly well understood if you use *ge*.

Some other measure words are:

'bottles'	*píng*	瓶
'tickets'	*piào*	张
'money'	*kuài*	块
'dog'	*tiáo*	条
'people'	*xiē*	些

So, if you want to say 'those people', you say *nèi*, 'those' and *rén*, 'people', but you must place *xie* the measure word between them. Those people is *Nèi xiē rén*.

Quantity

Some useful words to indicate quantity are:

all	*yīqiè*	一切
	quánbù	全部
	dōu	都
every	*měi yī ge*	每一个
enough	*gòu le*	够了
many, much	*duō*	多
little, few	*shǎo*	少
a bit	*yī diǎnr diǎnr*	一点点儿
several	*jǐ ge*	几十

Tense

To indicate completed action, you place the word *le* after the verb.

He is going to Shanghai.
Tā qù Shànghǎi. 他去上海

He has gone to Shanghai.
Tā qù le Shànghǎi. 他去了上海

If you want to show that something has happened (or hasn't happened) in the past, place the word *guò* directly after the verb.

He didn't go.
Tā méi qù. 他没去

He has never been.
Tā méi qù guò. 他没去过

The simplest way to indicate tense is by putting a time word in front of the verb. There is a list of these in the section called 'Telling the time'. Here are the three most useful words.

today	*jīntiān*	今天
tomorrow	*míngtiān*	明天
yesterday	*zuótiān*	昨天

Unlike in English, the verb itself does not change at all.

Commands

These words are usually emphasized.

Be quiet!	*Bié chǎo*	别吵
Go away!	*Zǒu kāi*	走开
Slow down!	*Màn zhe*	慢着
Stop!	*Tíng zhù*	停住

Some useful words

Adverbs

at once	*mǎshang*	马上
always	*lǎoshì*	老是
already	*yǐjīng*	已经
just now	*cái*	才
most	*zuì*	最
often	*jīngcháng*	经常
possibly	*kě néng*	可能
still	*hái*	还
still more	*gèng*	更
too	*tài*	太
very	*hěn*	很

Conjunctions

and	*hé, gēn*	和, 跟

after	*yǐ hòu*	以后
before	*yǐ qián*	以前
if	*yàoshì*	要是

Prepositions

about	*chàbuduō*	差不多
at	*zài*	在
because	*yīnwei*	因为
for	*wèi le*	为了
from (place)	*cóng . . . lái*	从 . . . 来
from (time)	*cóng . . . qǐ*	从 . . . 起
to (place)	*dào . . . qù*	到 . . . 去
to (time)	*dào*	到
towards	*wǎng*	往

Comparison

If you want to compare things, for example if you want to say that Shanghai is bigger than Beijing, you use the word *bi* between the two things you want to compare and then place the adjective after the whole phrase.

Shanghai (is) bigger than Beijing.

Shànghǎi bǐ Běijīng dà.　　上海比北京大

This (is) cheaper than that.

Zhèige bǐ nèi ge piányi.　　这个比那个便宜

Possession

To show ownership or possession, place the word *de* before the thing which is owned.

My dog.

Wǒ de gǒu.　　我的狗

Their room.

Tāmen de fángjiān.　　他们的房间

First Things

Names

It is the convention in China to place surnames, *xìng* before given names, *míng*. The surname usually consists of only one syllable, while the given name is usually made up of two. Thus Mao Zedong was Mr Mao to his colleagues and Zedong to his mummy and presumably to Madame Mao.

Surnames are usually made up of one syllable. Some of the most common ones are: Li, Wang, Huang, Zhang, Liu and Chen.

Given names are not selected from a list of 2,000 favourite Chinese boys and girls names. They are made up of one syllable words which stand for qualities which the Chinese parent would like to see developed in the child.

Questions and Requests

Where is, are ....
.... *zài nǎr*   在哪儿
Is, are there ....
Yǒu méiyǒu ....   有没有
Is this ....
Zhè shì bù shì ....   这是不是
What's this?
Zhè shì shénme?   这是什么
What must I do?
Wǒ yīnggāi zěnme yàng?   我应该怎么样
How far?
Duō yuǎn?   多远

15

16 First Things

I want ....
  Wǒ yào .... 我要

I should like ....
  Wǒ xiǎng yào .... 我想要

May I ....
  Wǒ néng bù néng .... 我能不能

An expression which seems to be very popular with Chinese bureaucracy is *bù fāngbiàn*, it's not convenient (Newspeak for 'It's not allowed').

Some useful phrases

I don't speak Chinese.
  Wǒ bù huì jiǎng Zhōngwén. 我不会讲中文

Do you speak English?
  Nǐ jiǎng Yīngyǔ ma? 你讲英语吗

Would you say that again please?
  Qǐng nǐ zài shuō yī biàn. 请你再说一遍

Please speak more slowly.
  Qǐng nǐ shuō de màn yīdiǎnr. 请你说得慢一点儿

Please point to the phrase in the book.
  Qǐng nǐ zài zhè běn shū lǐ zhǐchū yào 请你在这本书里指
  shuō de huà. 出要说的话

Let me see if I can find it in this book.
  Ràng wǒ kàn shū lǐ néng bù néng zhǎo 让我看书里能不能找到
  dào.

I understand.
  Wǒ dǒng. 我懂

I don't understand.
  Wǒ bù dǒng. 我不懂

What is written here?
  Zhèr xiě de shì shénme? 这儿写的是什么

Small Talk

It is very easy to strike up a conversation with Chinese you meet on your travels, so you might like to learn a few phrases which will enable you to tell people about yourself. Saying just a few words in Chinese can make a world of difference to the kind of response you get from people.

Just being foreign will make you a curiosity, and if you talk to the locals you will find that, initially, they all seem to want to know the same things about you: where you're from, your job, how much you earn, your age, whether or not you are married and how many children you have.

Nationality

I'm ....
  Wǒ shì .... 我是

Australian
  Àodàlìyà rén 澳大利亚人

American
  Měiguó rén 美国人

Canadian
  Jiānádà rén 加拿大人

Danish
  Dānmài rén 丹麦人

Dutch
  Hélán rén 荷兰人

English
  Yīngguó rén 英国人

French
 Fǎguó rén 法国人
German
 Déguó rén 德国人
Italian
 Yìdàlì rén 意大利人
Japanese
 Rìběn rén 日本人
Swedish
 Ruìdiǎn rén 瑞典人
Swiss
 Ruìshì rén 瑞士人
New Zealander
 Xīn Xīlán rén 新西兰人

Occupation

I'm ....
 Wǒ shì .... 我是
actor/actress
 yǎnyuán 演员
businessman
 shāng rén 商人
doctor
 yīshēng 医生
engineer
 gōngchéng shī 工程师
journalist
 jìzhě 记者
lawyer
 lǜshī 律师
student
 xuésheng 学生

teacher
jiàoshī 教师

writer
zuòjiā 作家

I'm in ....
Wǒ gǎo .... 我 搞

agriculture
nóngyè 农业

art
yìshù 艺术

construction
jiànzhù 建筑

music
yīnyuè 音乐

trade
màoyì 贸易

Family members

mother
mǔqin, māma 母亲，妈妈

father
fùqin, bàba 父亲，爸爸

son
érzi 儿子

daughter
nǚ er 女儿

elder brother
gēge 哥哥

younger brother
dìdi 弟弟

elder sister
jiějie 姐姐

younger sister
mèimei   妹妹
husband
àiren   爱人
wife
àiren   爱人

Some useful words and phrases

country
guójiā   国家
occupation
gōngzuò   工作
wage
gōngzī   工资
age
duōdà, suì   多大，岁
marry
jiéhūn   结婚
children
xiǎo háir   小孩儿
boy
nán háir   男孩儿
girl
nǚ háir   女孩儿

I get .... dollars a month.
Wǒ yī ge yuè yǒu .... kuài qián
gōngzī.   我一个月有 … 块钱工资
I'm .... years old.
Wǒ .... suì.   我 … 岁
(I'm) married.
Jié le.   结了

I have two children.
Wǒ yǒu liǎng ge xiǎo háir. 我有两个小孩儿
A boy and a girl.
Yī nán, yī nǚ 一男，一女
No, not yet.
Hái méiyǒu. 还没有

Greetings & Civilities

In addressing somebody they know well, the Chinese use the surname prefixed by *lǎo*, old, or *xiǎo*, young. It is perfectly all right for you to do the same. Since rank is very important in China, officials are usually addressed by their titles, although if you do not know what it is, don't worry too much.

Between strangers the all-purpose term is *tóngzhì*, comrade, but it's a bit archaic now. For people in positions which command respect (drivers are in this category), the term *shīfù* is commonly used. Strictly speaking, a *shīfù* is a skilled worker with apprentices under her or him, but this term is now used more extensively.

The Chinese don't say 'please' and 'thank you' quite as much as westerners, but you won't offend anyone if you stick to the type of politeness which is customary in your own country. For instance, contrary to what many people believe, it is not true that the Chinese would be offended if you thanked them for their hospitality.

When making a request it is nicer and more polite to start with the phrase *qǐng wèn* which is taken to mean 'please' or 'excuse me'. This expression is only used at the beginning of a sentence, and never at the end like 'please' in English would be used. You may hear *qǐng* used on its own. It is also an idiomatic expression which means 'after you'.

Yes (correct)
  duì

No (incorrect)
bù duì

不对

Thank you
xièxie

谢谢

Not at all
bù xiè

不谢

I'm sorry, Excuse me
duì bù qǐ

对不起

It doesn't matter
méi guānxi

没关系

Good, Fine, OK
hǎo

好

Good morning.
Zǎo.

早

How do you do?
Nǐ hǎo.

你好

Goodbye.
Zàijiàn.

再见

Good night.
Wǎn'ān.

晚安

See you tomorrow.
Míngtiān jiàn.

明天见

On Arrival

At the border

The Chinese call their country *Zhōnghuá Rénmín Gònghé Guó*, The People's Republic of China, or simply *Zhōngguó*, China.

Where is my luggage?
Wǒ de xíngli zài nǎr.   我的行李在哪儿

Where is the bus for .... hotel?
Qù .... lǚguǎn de gōnggōng qìchē zài nǎr?   去…旅馆的公共汽车在哪儿

Where can I get a taxi?
Zài nǎr jiào chūzū qìchē?   在哪儿叫出租汽车

What's the fare to .... ?
Qù .... yào duōshǎo qián?   去…要多少钱

Money

The local Chinese currency is called *Rénmínbì*, People's Currency. The money you are expected to be using is *wàihuì quàn*, foreign exchange certificates, or FECs. Officially, you are expected to use FECs, but there are situations, especially if you are travelling independently, where you will want to use local currency. The offical exchange rate is one to one, but, as there are 'luxury' stores, some Friendship stores for example, which will only accept FECs, there is a thriving black market.

Where can I change money?
Zài nǎr kěyǐ huàn qián?   在哪儿可以换钱

24

I'd like to change some ....
Wǒ xiǎng duìhuàn xiē ....   找想兑挼些

traveller's cheques
lǚxíng zhīpiào   旅行支票

Australian dollars
Àodàlìyà yuán   澳大利亚元

US dollars
Měi yuán   美元

pounds sterling
Yīng bàng   英镑

What is the exchange rate?
Duìhuàn lǜ shì duōshǎo?   兑换率是多少

Renminbi is based on the *yuán*. One yuan is made up of 10 *jiǎo* or 100 *fēn*. Jiao are sometimes called *máo*, and yuan are also known as *kuài*. Kuai is a measure word for money. The Chinese word which literally means money, as opposed to the name of the currency, is *qián*.

Some useful expressions

bank
yínháng   银行

credit card
xìnyòng kǎ   信用卡

signature
qiān míng   签名

small change
líng qián   零钱

Please let me have a receipt.
Qǐng kāi fāpiào.   请开发票

Haven't you made a mistake in the bill?
Nǐ bǎ zhàng suàn cuò le ba?   你把帐算错了吧

At the Hotel

If you are on a tour, and sometimes if you are not, you may want to use China Travel Service *Lǚxíngshè* to book you into a hotel. This will inevitably be a hotel reserved for foreigners. You can ask to share a dormitory, *sùshè*, where you just pay for the bed, which is naturally a lot cheaper. Most hotels not reserved for foreigners have dormitory accommodation, but you may have to insist on such accommodation here, otherwise the Chinese will assume you are another wealthy foreigner (and by their standards you are), and offer you a private or semi-private room.

There are a number of different types of hotel available.

a high class establishment for foreigners
bīnguǎn　　　　　宾馆
fàndiàn　　　　　饭店
lǚguǎn　　　　　旅馆
a guesthouse which may or may not
receive foreigners, and sometimes
used by high-ranking Chinese officials
　zhāodàisuǒ　　　招待所
a guesthouse, usually for native Chinese
and sometimes for overseas Chinese
　lǚshè　　　　　旅社

Though some hotels are more expensive than others, room charges are decided not by the class of accommodation so much as by the nationality of the guest. For the same room in the same establishment it is common practice to charge different rates depending on whether you are a foreign national (European, American, etc) an overseas Chinese, a Hong Kong Macao compatriot, or a Taiwan compatriot. Students, irrespective of nationality, get a cheaper rate, but you will be asked to show a student card.

Where is the ....
.... *zài nǎr.* 在哪儿

hotel
  lǚguǎn 旅馆

guesthouse
  zhāodàisuǒ 招待所

How far is it to the ....
  Qù .... duō yuǎn. 去...多远

hotel
  lǚguǎn 旅馆

guesthouse
  zhāodàisuǒ 招待所

I want ....
  .... *Wǒ yào ....* 我要

a single bed
  yī jiān dān rén fáng 一间单人房

a double bed
  yī jiān shuāng rén fáng 一间双人房

a suite
  yī jiān tào jiān 一间套间

to share a dorm
  zhù sùshè 住宿社

just a bed
  yī ge chuángwèi 一个床位

28 At the Hotel

I want a room with a ....
    Wǒ yào yī jiān dài .... de fángjiān 我要一间带…的房间

bathroom
    yùshì   浴室

shower
    línyù   淋浴

telephone
    diànhuà   电话

television
    diànshì   电视

window
    chuānghu   窗户

Is there ....
    Yǒu méiyǒu .... 有没有

air conditioning
    kōngtiáo shèbèi   空调设备

heating
    nuǎnqì   暖气

This room is too ....
    Zhè jiān fáng tài .... 这间房太

warm
    rè   热

cold
    lěng   冷

big
    dà   大

small
    xiǎo   小

dark
    àn   暗

noisy
chǎo 吵

Do you have .... room?
Yǒu méiyǒu .... de fángjiān? 有没有 … 的房间
another
qítā 其他
a cheaper
gèng piányi 更便宜
a better
gèng hǎo 更好

How much is .... ?
.... yào duōshǎo qián? 要多少钱
the room
zhù fáng 住房
just a bed
yǐ ge chuángwèi 一个床位
full board
bāo sān cān 包三餐

Some useful expressions

I am a student.
Wǒ shì xuésheng. 我是学生
Here is my student card.
Zhèi shì wǒ de xuésheng zhèng. 这是我的学生证
Your charges are too high.
Nǐmen shōu fèi tài gāo. 你们收费太高
Can you reduce your charges?
Shōu fèi néng jiǎn dī ma? 收费能减低吗
Please make up my bill.
Qǐng bǎ wǒ de zhàngdān kāi hǎo. 请把我的帐单开好

30 At the Hotel

Please wake me up at 6.30 am tomorrow.

Qǐng míngtiān zǎoshang liù diǎn bàn jiào xǐng wǒ.

请明天早上六点半叫醒我

In China, hotel keys, *yàoshi*, are usually left with the desk, *fúwù tái*, on each floor. You can ask at the desk for any services you may require.

The .... doesn't work.

   .... huài le.   坏了

light

   dēng   灯

air conditioner

   kōngtiáo   空调

tap (faucet)

   shuǐ lóngtóu   水龙头

shower (nozzle)

   liánpéng tóu   莲蓬头

toilet

   cèsuǒ   厕所

Can you get it repaired?

   Nǐ néng zhǎo rén xiū ma?   你能找人修吗

My room number is ....

   Wǒ .... hào fáng   我 ... 号房

May I have ....

   Wǒ néng yào .... ma?   我能要 ... 吗

some hangers

   jǐ ge guà yī jià   几个挂衣架

a plug adaptor

   ge diàn jiētóu   个电接头

some soap
  kuài féizào　　　　　　　　块 肥皂

If you need to make a telephone call overseas, make sure you book it well in advance.

Please put me through to ....　　请 给 我 接通 ...
  Qǐng gěi wǒ jiē tōng .... de diànhuà.　的 电话
the reception desk
  zǒng fúwù tái　　　　　　　总 服务台
room number ....
  .... hào fángjiān　　　　　...号房间
I want to make a long distance call.
  Wǒ yào dǎ ge chángtú diànhuà.　　我要打个长途电话
Will you please make a call to this number for me?
  Qǐng gěi wǒ jiē tōng zhèi ge diànhuà hào mǎ?　请 给 我 接通 这个 电话号码
The phone number at the other end is ....
  Duìfāng diànhuà hàomǎ shì ....　对方电话号码是...
Please make it a collect call.
  Qǐng yóu duìfāng fù kuǎn.　请 由 对方 付款

Food

On the whole Chinese cuisine, when eaten in China, is coarser, and more rough and ready than it is in Hong Kong, Taiwan and other Chinese communities in South-East Asia. Though the menu in some restaurants may run to over a hundred items, don't be surprised to find that the majority of these are unavailable. If you want a meal in a hurry the best thing would be to order a set menu. If offered western food, it is usually safe to agree to breakfast.

Some useful phrases

Do you have a menu in English?
Yǒu Yīngwén càidān ma?　有英文菜单吗

I am a vegetarian.
Wǒ chī sù de.　我吃素的

I like hot (spicy) food.
Wǒ ai chī là de.　我爱吃辣的

I don't like hot (spicy) food.
Wǒ bù ai chī là de.　我不爱吃辣的

This is stale.
Zhè ge bù xīnxiān.　这个不新鲜

This is not what I ordered.
Zhè ge bù shì wǒ diǎn de.　这个不是我点的

The bill please.
Qǐng jié zhàng.　请结帐

Please bring me ....
Qǐng lái ....　请来

a beer
  yī píng píjiǔ   一瓶啤酒
a bowl of rice
  yī wǎn fàn   一碗饭
two orders of sandwiches
  liǎng fèn sānmíngzhì   两份三明治

Restaurants serving local Chinese, as opposed to those catering for foreigners are very cheap, but many westerners have found the standard Chinese meal quite inedible.

In most towns there are small eating places selling snacks such as dumplings with meat and vegetable stuffing, or steamed buns with a savoury or sweet filling. These are usually sold by the *liǎng*, a unit of weight equal to 50 grams. There are also hawkers selling ices, noodles and cakes.

An everyday Chinese meal for two people consists of rice and/or steamed bread or plain noodles eaten with three or four dishes or meat and/or seafood and vegetables. Soup may be drunk with or at the end of the meal. It is not customary to serve dessert and you usually finish off with just fresh fruit and tea.

Many hotel restaurants simplify matters by offering a number of set menus differing in price. When ordering one of these you simply specify the price category you prefer.

The names of Chinese dishes range from the facy (Jade Velvet Chicken) to the straightforward (Chinese leek sauteed with shredded meat). When the kind of meat is not specified, pork is usually meant.

Meat

beef
  niú ròu   牛肉

chicken
jī 鸡

duck
yā 鸭

ham
huǒtuǐ 火腿

mutton
yáng ròu 羊肉

pork
zhū ròu 猪肉

Seafood

crab
xiè 蟹

fish
yú 鱼

prawns
xiā 虾

abalone
bàoyú 鲍鱼

shark's fins
yú chì 鱼翅

squid
yóuyú 鱿鱼

Vegetables

Shūcài 蔬菜

bamboo shoots
zhúsǔn 竹笋

beans
dòu 豆

Chinese cabbage
  báicài   白菜

cucumber
  huáng guā   黄瓜

eggplant
  qiézi   茄子

spring onions
  cōng   葱

tomatoes
  xīhóngshì   西红柿

Miscellaneous food

beancurd
  dòufu   豆腐

biscuits
  bǐnggān   饼干

bread
  miànbāo   面包

steamed buns
  bāozi   包子

butter
  huángyóu   黄油

cake
  dàngāo   蛋糕

dessert
  diǎnxīn   点心

dumplings
  jiǎozi   饺子

egg
  jī dàn   鸡蛋

ice-cream
  bīngqílín   冰淇淋

cold hors d'oevre
  lěng pánr 冷盤儿
noodles in soup
  tāng miàn 汤面
noodles (fried)
  chǎo miàn 炒面
pastry
  gāodiǎn 糕点
Chinese ravioli
  húntún 馄饨
soup
  tāng 汤
toast
  kǎo miànbāo piànr 烤面包片儿
yoghurt
  suān nǎi 酸奶

Spices
chilli
  làjiāo 辣椒
pepper
  hújiāo 胡椒
salt
  yán 盐
soya sauce
  jiàngyóu 酱油
sugar
  táng 糖
vinegar
  cù 醋

Cooking methods

braise
mèn　炯

broil
shāo　烧

casserole
shā guō　砂锅

curried
gālí　咖喱

deep fry
zhá　炸

fry
jiān　煎

roast
kǎo　烤

saute
chǎo　炒

steam
qīng zhēng　清蒸

Staples

steamed bread
mántou　馒头

steamed bread rolls
huājuǎnr　花卷儿

noodles
miàn tíao　面条

fried rice
chǎo fàn　炒饭

steamed rice
mǐfàn　米饭

Regional specialties
Peking duck
   Běijing kǎo yā 北京烤鸭
Mutton slices dipped in soup
   shuàn yáng ròu 涮羊肉
Moslem food
   qīngzhēn 清真

Alcoholic drinks
beer
   píjiǔ 啤酒
spirits
   bái jiǔ 白酒
wine
   pútao jiǔ 葡萄酒

Non-alcoholic drinks
coffee
   kāfēi 咖啡
fizzy drink
   qìshuǐ 汽水
milk
   niú nǎi 牛奶
mineral water
   kuàng quán shuǐ 矿泉水
orange juice
   júzi shuǐ 桔子水
tea
   chá shuǐ 茶水

Fruit

apples
píngguǒ 苹果

banana
xiāngjiāo 香蕉

fruit cocktail
shíjǐn shuǐguǒ 什锦水果

orange
júzi 桔子

peach
táozi 桃子

persimmon
shìzi 柿子

tangerine
gānjú 柑桔

water melon
xīguā 西瓜

Some useful words

ashtray
yān huī gāng 烟灰缸

bowl
wǎn 碗

breakfast
zǎo cān 早餐

chopsticks
kuàizi 筷子

cold
lěng 冷

cup
bēizi   杯子

dinner
wǎn fàn   晚饭

fork
chā   叉

hot
rè   热

knife
dāo   刀

lunch
zhōng fàn   中饭

plate
pánr   盘儿

restaurant
cāntīng, fànguǎn, fànzhuāng   餐厅, 饭馆, 饭庄

snack
xiǎo chī, diǎnxīn   小吃, 点心

spoon
chízi   匙子

table
zhuōzi   桌子

tumbler
shuǐbēi   水杯

toothpick
yá qiān   牙签

waiter/waitress
fúwù yuán   服务员

Some useful phrases
How much are the ....
     .... *duōshǎo qián*   …多少钱

I'll have ....
Yào ....

Shopping

In most big cities you will find it easiest to shop at the so-called Friendship Stores. These are department stores open only to foreigners and certain Chinese with special privileges. Apart from fully-owned state shops there are urban collectives providing services such as repairing shoes and sharpening knives, or serving meals and refreshments. At the 'free' markets you will find peasents offering a bizarre range of farm produce – anything from live turtles to tobacco leaf. In areas where shops are few, country fairs are sometimes held to offer newly rich peasents bicycle tyres, TV sets, nails, harnesses, furniture, clothing, farming utensils and so on.

Where is the ....?
　　....... *zài nǎr?*　　　　　　...在哪儿

Friendship Store
　　Yǒuyí shāngdiàn　　　　友谊商店

nearest department store
　　zuì jìn de bǎi huò shāngdiàn　最近的百货商店

best antique shop
　　zuì hǎo de gǔwán diàn　　最好的古玩店

nearest chemist
　　zuì jìn de yào diàn　　　最近的药店

free market
　　zìyóu shìchǎng　　　　　自由市场

country fair
　　wùzī jiāoliú huì　　　　　物资交流会

Here are some things you might run out of:

Where can I buy .... ?
  Zài nǎr néng mǎi dào .... ?　在哪儿能买到...

battery
  diànchí　电池

ballpoint pen
  yuán zhū bǐ　圆珠笔

cigarettes
  xiāngyān　香烟

envelopes
  xìn fēng　信封

film
  jiāojuǎnr　胶卷儿

face cream
  xuě huā gāo　雪花膏

flash bulbs
  shǎn guāng dēng　闪光灯

laces
  xié dài　鞋带

letter writing paper
  xìn zhǐ　信纸

matches
  huǒ chái　火柴

needle and thread
  zhēn xiàn　针线

postcards
  míng xìn piànr　明信片儿

razor blades
  tì dāo dāo piàn　剃刀刀片

sanitary towels
  wèishēng jīn　卫生巾

shampoo
 xǐ fà jì 洗发剂

soap
 féizào 肥皂

tooth brush
 yá shuā 牙刷

tooth paste
 yá gāo 牙膏

travelling bag
 lǚxíng bāo 旅行包

umbrella
 yǔ sǎn 雨伞

washing powder
 xǐ yī fěn 洗衣粉

Tourist shopping

arts and crafts
 gōngyì měishù 工艺美术

carpet
 dìtǎn 地毯

cashmere
 kāishìmǐ 开士米

ceramics
 táo qì 陶器

cloisonne
 jǐngtàilán 景泰蓝

fan
 shànzi 扇子

jade
 fěicuì 翡翠

jewellery
 zhūbǎo 珠宝

ivory
  xiàngyá　　　象牙

lacquerware
  qī qì　　　漆器

paintings
  huà　　　画

paper cuts
  jiǎn zhǐ　　　剪纸

porcelain
  cí qì　　　瓷器

silk
  zhēn sī　　　真丝

toys
  wán jù　　　玩具

Colours
black
  hēi (de)　　　黑 (的)

white
  bái (de)　　　白 (的)

blue
  lán (de)　　　蓝 (的)

green
  lǜ (de)　　　绿 (的)

red
  hóng (de)　　　红 (的)

yellow
  huáng (de)　　　黄 (的)

Some useful words
smaller
  xiǎo yīdiǎnr　　　小一点儿

bigger
  dà yìdiǎnr 大一点儿

cheaper
  gèng piányi 更便宜

expensive
  guì 贵

short
  duǎn 短

long
  cháng 长

Some useful phrases

Do you have .... ?
  Nǐ yǒu .... ma? 你有...吗

Just looking.
  Wǒ xiān kànkan. 我先看看

Do you have it in another colour/style?
  Yǒu biéde yánsè/yàngshì ma? 有别的颜色／样式吗

I like this one.
  Wǒ xǐhuan zhè ge. 我喜欢这个

How much is it?
  Duōshǎo qián? 多少钱

I don't understand.
  Wǒ bù dǒng. 我不懂

Please write it down.
  Qǐng xiě xià lái. 请写下来

Can you exchange this?
  Néng gěi wǒ huàn yī ge ma? 能给我换一个吗

Here is the receipt.
  Zhè shì shōujù. 这是收据

I'd like to return this.
Wǒ xiǎng bǎ zhè tuì huí. 我想把这退回

Please give me a refund
Qǐng bǎ qián tuì gěi wǒ. 请把钱退给我

Bargaining
The official word is that there is no bargaining in China. This is not the case when you get away from tour groups and Friendship Stores. Bargaining is alive and well in the markets and street stalls, as well as the Chinese hotels and restaurants.

May I bargain?
Néng jiǎng jià ma? 能讲价吗

Can you reduce the price?
Néng piányi yī diǎnr ma? 能便宜一点儿吗

Do you give a discount?
Néng dǎ zhékou ma? 能打折扣吗

It's too expensive.
Tài guì le. 太贵了

Around Town

In China, public transport is available in many forms. You can get around by bus, bicycle, taxi, hire car (complete with driver and guide), boat and train. Only Beijing has a subway system, called *Dìxià tiĕdào*, or *dì tiĕ* for short.

City maps are available from hotels, local bookstores and CITS offices, and the bus routes are clearly marked on them, although everything is usually in Chinese characters. These maps are called *shì qū dìtú* or *jiāotōng tú*. Before boarding a bus it might be a good idea to have someone write down the name of the place you want to go to in Chinese characters. You can show this to the driver or conductor.

The newer Chinese cities are laid out on a grid pattern, and part of the street name is usually the relevant compass point. The Chinese are apt to give directions in terms of the points of the compass too, rather than as left or right.

Directions

north
  bĕi   北

south
  nán   南

east
  dōng   东

west
  xī   西

straight ahead
  yī zhí zŏu   一直走

upstairs
lóu shàng 楼上

downstairs
lóu xià 楼下

right
yòu biānr 右边儿

left
zuǒ biānr 左边儿

Commands

Stop!
Tíng xiàlái 停下来

Slow down!
Màn zhe 慢着

Turn left
Guǎi zuǒ 拐左

Turn right
Guǎi yòu 拐右

Straight on
Yīzhí zǒu 一直走

Places to Visit

Please take me to ....
Qǐng bǎ wǒ dài dào .... qù 请把我带到 ... 去

bank
yínháng 银行

China Travel Service
Lǚxíngshè 旅行社

free markets
zìyóu shìchǎng 自由市场

memorial hall
jìniàn guǎn 纪念馆

monastery
 sì 寺
museum
 bówùguǎn 博物馆
park
 gōngyuán 公园
post office
 yóujú 邮局
theatre
 jùyuàn 剧院
temple
 miào 庙
university
 dàxué 大学
Please take me to the ....
 Qǐng nǐ dài wǒ qù kàn ...... 请你带我去看......
Peking opera
 jīng jù 京剧

Some useful phrases

Where is the nearest .... ?
 Zuì jìn de .... zài nǎr? 最近的...在哪儿
bus stop
 qì chē zhàn 汽车站
underground station
 dì tiě zhàn 地铁站
Which number bus shall I take
for ....?
 Qù .... děi zuò jǐ lù chē? 去...得坐几路车
Please tell me when we come to this
stop?
 Dào zhàn shí qǐng jiào wǒ. 到站时请叫我

Bargaining

I'd like to rent a bicycle.
Wǒ xiǎng zū yī liàng zìxíngchē. 我想租一辆自行车

How much is the rental?
Zū jīn yào duōshǎo? 租金要多少

I'll return it tomorrow.
Wǒ míngtiān huán nǐ. 我明天还你

How much is it per day?
Yī tiān duōshǎo qián? 一天多少钱

How much is the deposit?
Yājīn yào duōshǎo? 押金要多少

Where is the bicycle parking lot?
Zìxíngchē cúnfàng chù zài nǎr? 自行车存放处在哪儿

What time do you close?
Shénme shíhòu guān mén? 什么时候关门

At the post office

Your hotel will be able to take care of your post most of the time, but if you wish to use the post office, here is some help.

The Chinese address their letters by giving the name of the country first, then the city and then the street number. The name of the recipient comes last. If you forget this the post office is quite used to letters being addressed in *pinyin* the 'wrong' way round.

Where is the post office?
Yóujú zài nǎr? 邮局在哪儿

I'd like to buy some stamps.
Wǒ yào mǎi yóupiào. 我要买邮票

I want to send ....
Wǒ yào jì .... 我要寄

a letter
  yī fēng xìn　　　　　　一封信

a postcard
  yī zhāng míngxìnpiànr　　一张明信片

a parcel
  yī ge yóu bāo　　　　　　一个邮包

some printed matter
  yī xiē yìnshuā pǐn　　　　一些印刷品

Please send it ....
  Wǒ yào jì .... de　　　　我要寄…的

airmail
  hángkōng　　　　　　　　航空

surface mail
  píngyóu　　　　　　　　　平邮

express
  tè kuài　　　　　　　　　特快

registered
  guàhào　　　　　　　　　挂号

How much is it to .... ?
  Jì dào .... yào duōshǎo qián?　寄到…要多少钱

Australia
  Àodàlìyà　　　　　　　　澳大利亚

England
  Yīngguó　　　　　　　　　英国

United States
  Měiguó　　　　　　　　　美国

Some useful phrases
I want to send a telegram.
  Wǒ yào dǎ diànbào.　　　我要打电报

I want it to this place.
Wǒ yào dǎ dào zhè ge dìfang qù. 我要打到这个地方去

This is the name and address.
Zhè shì xìngmíng dìzhǐ. 这是姓名地址

Is there a poste restante?
Yǒu liú jú dài lǐng yóujiàn ma? 有当局特领邮件吗

Is there any mail for me?
Yǒu wǒ de xìn ma? 有我的信吗

My name is ....
Wǒ de míngzi shì .... 我的名字是

At the bank
Foreign currency

I want to change some ....
Wǒ xiǎng duì diǎn .... 我想兑点

American dollars
měijīn 美金

British pounds sterling
yīngbàng 英镑

Hong Kong currency
gǎngbì 港币

Canadian dollars, Australian dollars
jiābì, àobì 加币，澳币

Deutsche marks
mǎkè 马克

Some useful words

traveller's cheque
lǚxíng zhīpiào 旅行支票

bank draft
yínháng zhīpiào 银行支票

letter of credit
  xìnyòng zhèngmíng shū 信用证明书
cash
  xiànjīn, xiànkuǎn 现金, 现款

Some useful phrases

I would like to change some money.
  Wǒ yào huàn qián. 我要换钱

Where is the exchange?
  Duìhuànchu zai nar? 兑换处在哪儿

Where can I cash a traveller's cheque?
  Nǎr kěyǐ duìhuàn lǚxíng zhīpiào? 哪儿可以兑换旅行支票

Can you cash a personal cheque?
  Kěyǐ duìhuàn sīrén zhi piao ma? 可以兑换私人支票吗

I'm expecting some money from ....
  Wǒ zài děng cóng .... huìlái de yī bǐ
  qián. 我在等从 ... 汇来的一笔钱

Has it arrived yet?
  Yǐjing dào le ma? 已经到了吗

Please write it down.
  Qǐng nǐ xiě xiàlái. 请你写下来

In an emergency

I've lost ....
  Wǒ de .... yíshi le. 我的 ... 遗失了

my passport
  hùzhào 护照

my traveller's cheques
  lǚxíng zhīpiào 旅行支票

all my money
  qián dōu 钱都

Around the Country

Once you have a visa to enter China, you can travel to most big cities without any additional formalities, but if you want to go beyond these you have to have the permission of the Public Security Bureau, *gongan jú*. It is usually not a problem securing their permission, although there does seem to be some disagreement between different PSB offices as to what's open and what isn't. If you are in doubt, try another PSB office.

It is best to book train and long-distance bus tickets in advance. China Travel Service, *Lǚxíngshè*, located in most hotels, will do this for a fee.

Tickets

piào		票
hard seat		
yìng zuò		硬座
hard sleeper		
yìng wò		硬卧
soft seat		
ruǎn zuò		软座
soft sleeper		
ruǎn wò		软卧
single		
dān chéng		单程
return		
lái huí		来回

Some useful words

entrance
 rùkǒu 入口

exit
 chūkǒu 出口

platforms
 zhàntái 站台

first (train, bus etc)
 dìyībān 第一班

last
 mòbān 末班

next
 xià yī bān 下一班

By train

People's railway
 Rénmín tiělù 人民铁路

stopping train
 mànchē 慢车

fast train
 kuàichē 快车

express train
 tè kuàichē 特快车

left luggage office
 xíngli jìcún chù 行李寄存处

waiting room
 hòu chē shì 候车室

Some useful phrases

Where is the railway station?
 Huǒchē zhàn zài nǎr? 火车站在哪儿

Where is the ticket office?
Shòu piào chù zài nǎr? 售票处在哪儿

I'd like a ticket to ....
Wǒ xiǎng yào yī zhāng qù .... de pàio. 我想要一张去…的票

When does the train for .... leave?
Qù .... de huǒchē jǐ diǎn kai? 去…的火车几点开

Does this train stop at .... ?
Zhè cì huǒchē zài .... tíng ma? 这次火车在…停吗

Which platform does the train for .... leave from?
Qù .... de huǒchē cóng nǎ ge zhàntái chūfā? 去…的火车从哪个站台出发

Would you let me know before we get to .... ?
Dào .... qián qǐng nǐ gàosu wǒ hǎo ma? 到…前请你告诉我好吗

I've lost my ticket.
Wǒ de piào yíshī le. 我的票遗失了

Please, can you reroute my ticket?
Qǐng nǐ gěi wǒ qiānzhèng gǎi chéng? 请你给我签证改程

I'd like to return my ticket.
Wǒ xiǎng tùi piào. 我想退票

By long-distance bus

Where is the long-distance bus station?
Chángtú qìchē zhàn zài nǎr? 长途汽车站在哪儿

When does the bus for .... leave?
Qù .... de qìchē jǐ diǎn kāi? 去…的汽车几点开

Where can I get a bus to .... ?
Wǒ dào nǎr chéng qù .... de chángtú qìchē? 我到哪儿乘去…的长途汽车

By air

Where is the Chinese airline booking office?

Zhōngguó mín háng bànshì chù zài nǎr? 中国民航办事处在哪儿

Which flight is it?

Shì nǎ yī cì hángbān? 是哪一次航班

I'd like to buy a ticket to ....

Wǒ yào yīzhāng qù .... de piào. 我要一张去…的票

When does it arrive in .... ?

Shénme shíhòu dào dá .... ? 什么时候到达

When does the flight take off?

Fēijī jǐ diǎn qǐfēi? 飞机几点起飞

What time do I have to check in?

Wǒ yīnggāi jǐdiǎn dào jīchǎng bànlǐ dēngjì shǒuxù? 我应该几点到机场办理 登记手续

In the Countryside
Some useful words

countryside

nóngcūn, xiāng xià 农村, 乡下

commune

gōngshè 公社

grottoes

shíkū 石窟

province

shěng 省

ruins

yízhǐ 遗址

scenery
  fēngjǐng 风景

swimming
  yóuyǒng 游泳

bridge
  qiáo 桥

hill
  shān 山

lake
  hú 湖

pagoda
  tǎ 塔

river
  jiāng, hé 江, 河

road
  lù 路

street
  jiē 街

Some useful phrases

When does it open?
  Shénme shíhòu kāi? 什么时候开

It's raining
  Xià yǔ le. 下雨了

It's snowing
  Xià xuě le. 下雪了

I'm lost.
  Wǒ mílù le. 我迷路了

Where is the .... Embassy?
  .... dàshǐguǎn zài nǎr? ..大使馆在哪儿

Australian
  Àodàlìyà 澳大利亚

American
Měiguó 美国

Canadian
Jiānádà 加拿大

Danish
Dānmài 丹麦

Dutch
Hélán 荷兰

French
Fǎguó 法国

German
Déguó 德国

Italian
Yìdàlì 意大利

Swedish
Ruìdiǎn 瑞典

Swiss
Ruìshì 瑞士

New Zealand
Xīn Xīlán 新西兰

Places
Provinces
Anhui 安徽
Fujian 福建
Gansu 甘肃
Guangdong 广东
Guangxi 广西
Guizhou 贵州
Heilongjiang 黑龙江
Henan 河南
Hebei 河北

Hunan	湖南
Hubei	湖北
Jiangxi	江西林
Jilin	吉林
Nei Menggu (Inner Mongolia)	内蒙古
Ningxia	宁夏
Liaoning	辽宁
Qinghai	青海西
Shaanxi	陕西
Shandong	山东
Shanxi	山西
Sichuan	四川
Taiwan	台湾
Xinjiang	新疆
Xizang (Tibet)	西藏
Yunnan	云南
Zhejiang	浙江

Cities

Anshan	鞍山
Beijing	北京
Changchun	长春
Changsha	长沙
Chongqing	重庆
Dalian	大连
Daqing	大庆
Datong	大同
Dazhai	大寨
Hangzhou	杭州
Ha'erbin	哈尔滨
Jinan	济南
Kunming	昆明

Guangzhou	广州
Guilin	桂林
Luoyang	洛阳
Nanjing	南京
Nanning	南宁
Qingdao	青岛
Shanghai	上海
Shaoshan	韶山
Shenyang	沈阳
Shijiazhuang	石家庄
Suzhou	苏州
Tianjin	天津
Wuhan	武汉
Wulumuqi (Urumchi)	乌鲁木齐
Wuxi	无锡
Xian	西安
Yanan	延安
Zhengzhou	郑州

Health

If you fall ill during your trip you can ask to be treated by either western medicine, *xi yi*, or Chinese traditional medicine, *zhong yi*, or a combination of the two.

I have ....
   wǒ ....   我

a fever
   fā shāo le   发烧了

flu
   gǎnmào le   感冒了

diarrhoea
   xiè dùzi   泻肚子

indigestion
   xiāohuà bù liáng   消化不良

constipation
   dàbiàn bù tōng   大便不通

cramps
   chōu jīn   抽筋

asthma
   yǒu qìchuǎn bìng   有气喘病

I have ....
   Wǒ huàn ....   我患

cholera
   huòluàn   霍乱

dysentery
   lìji   痢疾

hepatitis
  gān yán 肝炎

malaria
  nüèji 疟疾

tetanus
  pòshāngfēng 破伤风

typhoid
  shānghán 伤寒

I'm allergic to ....
  Wǒ duì .... guò mǐn. 我对…过敏

antibiotics
  kàngshēngsù 抗生素

penicillin
  qīngméisù 青霉素

My .... hurts.
  Wǒ .... téng. 我…疼

head
  tóu 头

throat
  hóulóng 喉咙

tooth
  yá 牙

stomach
  wèi 胃

Treatment

acupuncture
  zhēnjiǔ 针灸

antibiotics
  kàngshēngsù 抗生素

hospital
  yīyuàn　医院

injection
  dǎ zhēn　打针

prescription
  kāi yàofāng　开药方

rest
  xiūxi　休息

sleeping pills
  an mián yào　安眠药

surgery
  dòng shǒushù　动手术

fill a tooth
  bǔ yá　补牙

extract a tooth
  bá yá　拔牙

Some useful words

bleed
  chū xué　出血

burn
  tàng shāng　烫伤

food poisoning
  shí wù zhòng dú　食物中毒

inflammation
  fāyán　发炎

rash
  zhěnzi　疹子

ulcer
  kuìyáng　溃疡

wound
  shāngkǒu　伤口

Some useful phrases

I have a pain here.

Wǒ zhèr téng. 我这儿疼

I don't feel well.

Wǒ bù shūfu. 我不舒服

I'm ill.

Wǒ bìng le. 我病了

Please get me a doctor at once.

Qǐng mǎshàng gěi wǒ qǐng yī wèi dàifu lái. 请马上给我请一位大夫来

I want to see a doctor.

Wǒ yào kàn yīshēng. 我要看医生

An English speaking one.

Zuì hǎo néng shuō Yīngyǔ de. 最好能说英语的

I have broken my glasses.

Wǒ bǎ wǒ de yǎnjìng nòng huài le. 我把我的眼镜弄坏了

At the Chemist

chemist

yào diàn 药店

I'd like something for ....

Wǒ yào yī xiē zhì .... de yào. 我要一些治...的药

Take it three times a day.

Měi tiān fú sān cì. 每天服三次

Please give me some ....

Qǐng gěi wǒ .... 请给我...

aspirin

āsīpǐlín 阿司匹林

antiseptic cream

kàng jūn gāo 抗菌膏

bandages

bēngdài 绷带

cough drops
késòu táng 咳嗽糖
disinfectant
qīng dú jì 清毒剂
eye drops
yǎn yào shuǐ 眼药水

In an emergency

Help!
Jiù rén a 救人啊
Danger!
Wēixiǎn 危险
Call the police!
Jiào jǐngchá 叫警察
Get help quickly!
Kuài zhǎo rén bāngmáng 快找人帮忙
There has been an accident.
Fāshēng shìgù le. 发生事故了

Time & Dates

What time is it?
  Xiànzài jǐdiǎn le?　　　　现在几点了

early morning
  zǎoshang　　　　早上

morning
  shàngwǔ　　　　上午

midday
  zhongwu　　　　中午

afternoon
  xiàwǔ　　　　下午

evening
  wǎnshang　　　　晚上

night
  yèli　　　　夜里

9 am
  zǎoshang jiǔ diǎn　　　　早上九点

12 noon
  zhōngwǔ shí'èr diǎn　　　　中午十二点

1.25 pm
  xiàwǔ yī diǎn èrshí wǔ fēn　　　　下午一点二十五分

2.30 pm
  xiàwǔ liǎng diǎn bàn　　　　下午两点半

Some useful words
hour
  xiǎoshí　　　　小时

68

minute
  fēn zhōng 分钟
second
  miǎo zhōng 秒钟
half an hour
  bàn xiǎoshí 半小时
quarter of an hour
  yī kè zhōng 一刻钟

Present

today
  jīntiān 今天
this week
  zhè ge xīngqī 这个星期
this month
  zhè ge yuè 这个月
this year
  jīn nián 今年
immediately
  mǎshàng 马上
now
  xiànzài 现在

Past

yesterday
  zuótiān 昨天
last week
  shàng ge xīngqī 上个星期
last month
  shàng ge yuè 上个月
last year
  qù nián 去年

Future

tomorrow
  míngtiān　　　　　明天

day after tomorrow
  hòu tiān　　　　　后天

next week
  xià ge xīngqī　　下个星期

next month
  xià ge yuè　　　下个月

next year
  míng nián　　　　明年

in the morning
  zǎoshang　　　　早上

in the afternoon
  xiàwǔ　　　　　　下午

in the evening
  wǎnshang　　　　晚上

within .... days
  .... tiān nèi　　...天内

In Chinese, dates are written with the year and the month
preceding the number of the day: *yī jiǔ bā sì nián shí yuè yī rì*
or 1-9-8-4-year-10-month-1-day is really 1 October 1984.

one year
  yī nián　　　　　一年
one month
  yī ge yuè　　　　一个月
one week
  yī ge xīngqī　　　一个星期
one day
  yī tiān　　　　　一天

Days of the Week

Monday
xīngqī yī 星期 一

Tuesday
xīngqī èr 星期 二

Wednesday
xīngqī sān 星期 三

Thursday
xīngqī sì 星期 四

Friday
xīngqī wǔ 星期 五

Saturday
xīngqī liù 星期 六

Sunday
xīngqī tiān 星期 天

Months

January
yī yuè 一 月

February
èr yuè 二 月

March
sān yuè 三 月

April
sì yuè 四 月

May
wǔ yuè 五 月

June
liù yuè 六 月

July
qī yuè 七 月

August
  bā yuè   八 月
September
  jiŭ yuè   九 月
October
  shí yuè   十 月
November
  shíyī yuè   十一月
December
  shí'èr yuè   十二月

Chinese Dynasties

In China historical time is marked by dynasties. When you go sightseeing you are likely to come across references to them.

2100 – 1600 BC
  Xià   夏
1600 – 1100 BC
  Shāng   商
Western Zhou 1100 – 771 BC
  Xī Zhōu   西周
Spring – Autumn period 770-476 BC
  Chūn qiū   春秋
Warring states period 475 – 221 BC
  Zhàn guó   战国
221 – 207 BC
  Qín   秦
Western Han 206 BC – 24 AD
  Xi Hàn   西汉
Eastern Han 25 – 220 AD
  Dōng Hàn   东汉

Three Kingdoms period, 220 – 265
  Sān guó   三国

Western Jin 265 – 316
  Xī Jìn   西晋

Eastern Jin 317 – 420
  Dōng Jìn   东晋

Southern and northern dynasties period
420 – 582
  Nán běi cháo   南北朝

581 – 618
  Suí   隋

618 – 907
  Táng   唐

Five dynasties period 907 – 960
  Wǔdài   五代

916 – 1125
  Liáo   辽

960 – 1279
  Sòng   宋

1125 – 1234
  Jīn   金

1271 – 1368
  Yuán   元

1368 – 1644
  Míng   明

1644 – 1911
  Qīng   清

Numbers

Chinese counting is based on the decimal system. The 'teens' are counted by adding the appropriate number to 10 (e.g. eleven is $10 + 1$, 19 is $10 + 9$). From 20 on the numbers are counted in multiples of 10. In this way 20 is *ershi*, which is two-ten, 40 is *sishi* or four-ten, 66 is *liushi liu* or six-ten six.

0
  líng   零
1
  yī   一
2
  èr   二
3
  sān   三
4
  sì   四
5
  wŭ   五
6
  liù   六
7
  qī   七
8
  bā   八
9
  jiŭ   九

10
  shí   十

11
  shíyī   十 一

12
  shí'èr   十 二

13
  shí'sān   十 三

20
  èrshí   二 十

21
  èrshí yī   二 十 一

22
  èrshí èr   二 十 二

23
  èrshí sān   二 十 三

30
  sānshí   三 十

31
  sānshí yī   三 十 一

40
  sìshí   四 十

50
  wǔshí   五 十

60
  liùshí   六 十

70
  qīshí   七 十

80
  bāshí   八 十

90
  jiǔshí   九 十

100
  yī bǎi   一百
101
  yī bǎi líng yī   一百零一
102
  yī bǎi líng èr   一百零二
110
  yī bǎi yī shí   一百一十
189
  yī bǎi bāshí jiǔ   一百八十九
200
  liǎng bǎi/èr bǎi   两百 / 二百
300
  sān bǎi   三百
1,000
  yī qiān   一千
1,367
  yī qiān sān bǎi liùshí qī 一千三百六十七
10,000
  yī wàn   一万
50,000
  wǔ wàn   五万
100,000
  shí wàn   十万
1,000,000
  yī bǎi wàn   一百万
100,000,000
  yīyì   一亿

Cardinal Numbers
first
  dì yī   第一

second
  dì èr　第二
third
  dì sān　第三
tenth
  dì shí　第十

Ordinal Numbers
once
  yī cì　一次
twice
  liǎng cì　两次
three times
  sān cì　三次
double
  liǎng bèi　两倍
triple
  sān bèi　三倍

Some useful words
half a ....
  bàn ge　半个
a quarter
  sì fēn zhī yī　四分之一
three-quarters
  sì fēn zhī sān　四分之三
about
  .... *zuǒyòu*　...左右
enough
  zúgòu　足够
number
  hàomǎ　号码

kilometre
  gōnglǐ   公里
mile
  lǐ   哩
foot (12 inches)
  chǐ   尺
millimetre
  háomǐ   毫米
inch
  cùn   寸

Vocabulary

A

about – .... *zuǒyòu* 左右
accident – *shìgù* 事故
actor/actress – *yǎnyuán* 演员
acupuncture – *zhēnjiǔ* 针灸
address – *dìzhǐ* 地址
aeroplane – *fēijī* 飞机
afternoon – *xiàwǔ* 下午
age – *suì* 岁
agriculture – *nóngyè* 农业
air-conditioning – *kōngtíao* 空调
airmail – *hángkōng* 航空
all – *dōu* 都
allergic – *guòmín* 过敏
antibiotics – *kàngshēngsù* 抗生素
antique – *gǔwán* 古玩
antiseptic cream – *kāng jūn gāo* 抗菌膏
apples – *píngguǒ* 苹果
art – *yìshù* 艺术
arts & crafts – *gōngyì měishù* 工艺美术
ashtray – *yān huī gāng* 烟灰缸
aspirin – *āsīpǐlín* 阿司匹林
asthma – *qìchuǎn bìng* 气喘病

B

banana – *xiāngjiāo* 香蕉

79

ballpoint – *yuán zhū bǐ* 圆珠笔

bandages – *bēngdài* 绷带

bank – *yínháng* 银行

bathroom – *yùshì* 浴室

batteries – *diànchí* 电池

beancurd – *dòufu* 豆腐

bed – *chuáng* 床

beef – *niú ròu* 牛肉

beer – *píjiǔ* 啤酒

bicycle – *zìxíngchē* 自行车

big – *dà* 大

bill – *zhàngdān* 帐单

biscuits – *bǐnggān* 饼干

blankets – *tǎnzi* 毯子

bleed – *chū xuě* 出血

book – *shū* 书

bottle – *píng* 瓶

bowl – *wǎn* 碗

boy – *nán háir* 男孩儿

bread – *miànbāo* 面包

breakfast – *zǎo cān* 早餐

bridge – *qíao* 桥

broken – *huài le* 坏了

building/construction – *jiànzhù* 建筑

burn – *tàng shāng* 烫伤

bus stop – *qìchē zhàn* 汽车站

businessman – *shāng rén* 商人

butter – *huángyóu* 黄油

buy – *mǎi*

C

cake – *dàngāo* — 蛋糕

can/cannot – *néng/bù néng* — 能/不能

carpet – *dìtǎn* — 地毯

ceramics – *táo qì* — 陶器

change (money) – *duìhuàn* — 兑换

cheap – *piányi* — 便宜

chemist's (drugstore) – *yào diàn* — 药店

chicken – *jī* — 鸡

child – *xiǎo háir* — 小孩儿

chilli – *làjiāo* — 辣椒

chopsticks – *kuàizi* — 筷子

cigarettes – *xiāngyān* — 香烟

cloisonne – *jǐngtàilán* — 景泰蓝

closed – *bù kāifàng* — 不开放

coat hangers – *guà yī jià* — 挂衣架

coffee – *kāfēi* — 咖啡

cold – *lěng* — 冷

colour – *yánsè* — 颜色

come (v) – *lái* — 来

commune – *gōngshè* — 公社

comrade – *tóngzhì* — 同志

constipation – *dàbiàn bù tōng* — 大便不通

correct (yes) – *duì* — 对

cough drops – *késòu táng* — 咳嗽糖

country – *guójiā* — 国家

countryside – *nóngcūn/xiāng xià* — 农村/乡下

county seat – *xiàn chéng* — 县城

crab – *xiè* — 蟹

cramps – *chōu jīn* 抽筋
credit card – *xìn yòng kǎ* 信用卡
cup – *bēizi* 杯子

D

dark – *àn* 暗
dessert – *diǎnxīn* 点心
diabetes – *tángniàobìng* 糖尿病
diarrhoea – *xiè dùzi* 泻肚子
dining car – *cān chē* 餐车
dinner – *wǎn fàn* 晚饭
disinfectant – *qīng dú jì* 清毒剂
doctor – *dàifu/yīshēng* 大夫 / 医生
dormitory – *sùshè* 宿舍
duck – *yā* 鸭
dumplings – *jiǎozi* 饺子

E

east – *dōng* 东
eat (v) – *chī* 吃
egg – *jī dàn* 鸡蛋
electric fan – *diàn fēngshàn* 电风扇
embassy – *dàshǐguǎn* 大使馆
engineer – *gōngchéng shī* 工程师
enough – *zúgòu* 足够
envelopes – *xìn fēng* 信封
evening – *wǎnshang* 晚上
exchange – *huàn* 换
exchange rate – *duìhuàn lǜ* 兑换率
express – *tè kuài/jiā jí* 特快 / 加急
eye drops – *yǎn yào shuǐ* 眼药水

F

face cream – *xuě huā gāo*   雪花膏
faint – *tóu hūn*   头昏
fan – *shànzi*   扇子
far – *yuǎn*   远
fetch (meet) – *jiē*   接
fever – *fā shāo*   发烧
film – *jiāojuǎnr*   胶卷儿
find – *zhǎo*   找
fish – *yú*   鱼
fizzy drink – *qì shuǐ*   汽水
flash bulbs – *shǎn guāng dēng*   闪光灯
flight – *hángbān*   航班
'flu – *gǎnmào*   感冒
food poisoning – *shí wù zhòng dú*   食物中毒
foreign currency certificates – *wàihuì quàn*   外汇券
fork – *chā*   叉
free markets – *zìyóu shìchǎng*   自由市场
fruit cocktails – *shíjǐn shuǐguǒ*   什锦水果

G

girl – *nǚ háir*   女孩儿
glasses (spectacles) – *yǎnjìng*   眼镜
go – *qù*   去
good – *hǎo*   好
goodbye – *zài jiàn*   再见
grottoes – *shíkū*   石窟

H

ham – *huǒtuǐ* 火腿
head – *tóu* 头
heating – *nuǎn qì* 暖气
help (v) – *bāngmāng* 帮忙
here – *zhèr* 这儿
hill – *shān* 山
hors-d'oeuvre – *léng pánr* 冷整儿
hospital – *yīyuàn* 医院
hot – *rè* 热
hotel – *lǚguǎn* 旅馆
hour – *xiǎoshí* 小时
how – *zénme* 怎么

I

ice cream – *bīngqílín* 冰淇淋
immediately – *mǎshàng* 马上
indigestion – *xiāohuà bù liáng* 消化不良
inflammation – *fāyán* 发炎
injection – *dǎ zhēn* 打针
ivory – *xiàng yá* 象牙

J

jade – *fěicuì* 翡翠
jewellery – *zhūbǎo* 珠宝
journalist – *jìzhě* 记者

K

key – *yàoshi* 钥匙
kilogrammes – *gōngjīn* 公斤

kilometres – *gōnglǐ* 公里

knife – *dāo* 刀

L

lacquerware – *qī qì* 漆器

lake – *hú* 湖

lawyer – *lǜshī* 律师

left – *zuǒ biānr* 左边儿

letter – *xìn* 信

letter-writing paper – *xìn zhǐ* 信纸

like (v) – *xǐhuan* 喜欢

long-distance – *chángtú* 长途

look – *kàn* 看

luggage – *xíngli* 行李

lunch – *zhōng fàn* 中饭

M

map – *dìtú* 地图

marry – *jiéhūn* 结婚

matches – *huǒchái* 火柴

memorial hall – *jìniàn guǎn* 纪念馆

menu – *càidān* 菜单

milk – *niú nǎi* 牛奶

mineral water – *kuàng quán shuǐ* 矿泉水

minutes – *fēn zhōng* 分钟

monastery – *sì* 寺

money – *qián* 钱

months – *yuè* 月

morning – *zǎoshang* 早上

music – *yīnyuè* 音乐

museum – *bówùguǎn* 博物馆

Muslim – *Qīngzhēn* 清真

mutton – *yáng ròu* 羊肉

N

name – *xìngmíng* 姓名

near – *jìn* 近

needle – *zhēn* 针

noisy – *chǎo* 吵

noodles – *miàn tiáo* 面条

north – *běi* 北

now – *xiànzài* 现在

number – *hàomǎ* 号码

O

old – *lǎo* 老

open – *kāi* 开

or – *háishì* 还是

orange – *júzi* 桔子

orange juice – *júzi shuǐ* 桔子水

other – *biéde/qítā* 别的 / 其他

P

pagoda – *tǎ* 塔

pain – *téng* 疼

paintings – *huà* 画

paper cuts – *jiǎn zhǐ* 剪纸

parcel – *yóu bāo* 邮包

park – *gōngyuán* 公园

passport – *hùzhào* 护照

peach – *táozi* 桃子

pepper – *hújiāo* 胡椒

peppery hot – *là* 辣

persimmon – *shìzi* 柿子

place of work – *dānwèi* 单位

plate – *pánr* 盘儿

platform – *zhàntái* 站台

plug adaptor – *diàn jiētóu* 电接头

police – *jǐngchá* 警察

porcelain – *cí qì* 瓷器

pork – *zhū ròu* 猪肉

post (v) – *jì* 寄

post office – *yóujú* 邮局

postcards – *míngxìnpiànr* 明信片儿

prawns – *xiā* 虾

prescription – *yào fāng* 药方

printed matter – *yìnshuā pǐn* 印刷品

province – *shěng* 省

R

railway – *tiělù* 铁路

rain (v) – *xià yǔ* 下雨

rash – *zhěnzi* 疹子

ravioli – *húntún* 馄饨

razor blades – *tì dāo dāo piàn* 剃刀刀片儿

receipt – *fāpiào/shōujù* 发票/收据

reception desk – *fúwù tái* 服务台

registered – *guàhào* 挂号

rent/hire – *zū* 租

repair – *xiū* 修

rest – *xiūxi* 休息

restaurant – *cāntīng, fànguǎn* 餐厅, 饭馆

return (goods) – *tuì* 退
rice – *mǐfàn* 米饭
right (side) – *yòu biānr* 右边儿
river – *jiāng/hé* 江 / 河
road – *lù* 路
room – *fángjiān* 房间
ruins – *yízhǐ* 遗址

S

salt – *yán* 盐
sandwiches – *sānmíngzhì* 三明治
sanitary towels – *wèishēng jīn* 卫生巾
scenery – *fēngjǐng* 风景
seconds – *miǎo zhōng* 秒钟
shampoo – *xǐ fà jì* 洗发剂
shoe laces – *xié dài* 鞋带
shop – *shāngdiàn* 商店
shower – *línyù* 淋浴
signature – *qiān míng* 签名
silk – *zhēn sī* 真丝
sleeping pills – *ān mián yào* 安眠药
slow – *màn* 慢
small – *xiǎo* 小
small change – *líng qián* 零钱
smoke (v) – *chōu yān* 抽烟
snack – *diǎnxīn* 点心
snow (v) – *xià xuě* 下雪
soap – *féizào* 肥皂
soup – *tāng* 汤
south – *nán* 南
soya sauce – *jiàngyóu* 酱油

speak (v) – *jiǎng/shuō* 讲 / 说
spoon – *chízi* 匙子
stale – *bù xīnxiān* 不新鲜
stamps – *yóupiào* 邮票
steamed bread – *mántou* 馒头
steamed bread rolls –
  huājuǎnr 花卷儿
stomach – *dùzi* 肚子
stop (v) – *tíng* 停
street – *jiē* 街
student – *xuésheng* 学生
style – *yàngshì* 样式
sugar – *táng* 糖
suite – *tàojiān* 套间
surface mail – *píngyóu* 平邮
surgery – *dòng shǒushù* 动手术
sweet – *tián* 甜
swimming – *yóuyǒng* 游泳

T
table – *zhuōzi* 桌子
tangerine – *gānjú* 柑桔
tap – *shuǐ lóngtóu* 水龙头
teacher – *jiàoshī* 教师
telegram – *diànbào* 电报
telephone – *diànhuà* 电话
tell – *gàosu* 告诉
temple – *miào* 庙
thanks – *xièxie* 谢谢
theatre – *jùyuàn* 剧院
there – *nàr* 那儿
thread – *xiàn* 线

throat – *hóulóng* 喉咙

tickets – *piào* 票

ticket office – *shòu piào chù* 售票处

toast – *kǎo miànbāo piànr* 烤面包片儿

today – *jīntiān* 今天

toilet – *cèsuǒ* 厕所

tomorrow – *míngtiān* 明天

tooth – *yá* 牙

tooth brush – *yá shuā* 牙刷

toothpick – *yá qiān* 牙签

toys – *wánjù* 玩具

trade – *màoyì* 贸易

train – *huǒchē* 火车

travel – *lǔxíng* 旅行

traveller's cheques – *lǔxíng zhīpiào* 旅行支票

travelling bag – *lǔxíng bāo* 旅行包

tumbler – *shuǐ bēi* 水杯

U

ulcer – *kuìyáng* 溃疡

umbrella – *yǔ sǎn* 雨伞

underground (subway) – *dìxià tiědào* 地下铁道

understand – *dǒng* 懂

university – *dàxué* 大学

upstairs – *lóu shàng* 楼上

V

vegetables – *shūcài* 蔬菜

vegetarian – *chī sù* 吃素

village fair – *wùzī jiāoliú huì* 物资交流会

vinegar – *cù* 醋

vomit – *ǒutù* 呕吐

W

waiter/waitress – *fúwù yuán* 服务员

wage – *gōngzī* 工资

wait (v) – *děng* 等

wake (v) – *jiào xǐng* 叫醒

want (v) – *yào* 要

washing powder – *xǐ yī fěn* 洗衣粉

watermelon – *xīguā* 西瓜

weather/climate – *tiānqì* 天气

week – *xīngqī* 星期

west – *xī* 西

what – *shénme* 什么

when – *shénme shíhòu* 什么时候

where – *nǎr* 哪儿

which – *nǎ yī ge* 哪一个

who – *shéi* 谁

wine – *pútao jiǔ* 葡萄酒

work – *gōngzuò* 工作

wound – *shāngkǒu* 伤口

writer – *zuòjiā* 作家

Y

year – *nián* 年

yesterday – *zuótiān* 昨天

yoghurt – *suān nǎi* 酸奶

young – *xiǎo* 小

Lonely Planet travel guides

Africa on a Shoestring
Australia – a travel survival kit
Alaska – a travel survival kit
Bali & Lombok – a travel survival kit
Bangladesh – a travel survival kit
Burma – a travel survival kit
Bushwalking in Papua New Guinea
Canada – a travel survival kit
China – a travel survival kit
Ecuador & the Galapagos Islands
Hong Kong, Macau & Canton – a travel survival kit
India – a travel survival kit
Japan – a travel survival kit
Kashmir, Ladakh & Zanskar – a travel survival kit
Kathmandu & the Kingdom of Nepal
Korea & Taiwan – a travel survival kit
Malaysia, Singapore & Brunei – a travel survival kit
Mexico – a travel survival kit
New Zealand – a travel survival kit
North-East Asia on a Shoestring
Pakistan – a travel survival kit kit
Papua New Guinea – a travel survival kit
The Philippines – a travel survival kit
South America on a Shoestring
South-East Asia on a Shoestring
Sri Lanka – a travel survival kit
Tahiti – a travel survival kit
Thailand – a travel survival kit
Tramping in New Zealand
Travel with Children
Travellers Tales
Trekking in the Indian Himalaya
Trekking in the Nepal Himalaya
Turkey – a travel survival kit
USA West
West Asia on a Shoestring

Lonely Planet phrasebooks

Indonesia Phrasebook
China Phrasebook
Nepal Phrasebook
Thailand Phrasebook